I like to stop at the pet store.
I like to look at the pets.

2

Some pets have spots.
I have spots on my face.

Some pets sniff and smell a lot.
I use my nose to sniff and smell.

3

4

Some pets have a shell.
I use a shell when I ride my bike.

Some pets can swim.
I can swim in the lake.

5

6

Some pets like to sleep a lot.
I sleep in a bed.

Some pets can speak.
I can speak.

7

8

Some pets have scales.
Snakes have scales.
A snake gets rid of its skin.
But I like my skin as it is!